WITHDRAWN

3/04

Cornerstones of Freedom

The Story of
HARRIET BEECHER STOWE

By Maureen Ash

CHILDRENS PRESS®
CHICAGO

This illustration, entitled *Separation of Mother and Child*, by George Cruickshank, appeared in the first British edition of *Uncle Tom's Cabin*.

Library of Congress Cataloging-in-Publication Data

Ash, Maureen.

  The story of Harriet Beecher Stowe / by Maureen Ash.
    p.   cm. — (Cornerstones of freedom)
  Summary: Describes the life and work of the woman whose famous book "Uncle Tom's Cabin" had a great impact on the slavery situation in the United States.
  ISBN 0-516-04746-9
  1. Stowe, Harriet Beecher, 1811-1896—Biography—Juvenile literature. 2. Authors, American—19th century—Biography—Juvenile literature.
3. Abolitionists—United States—Biography—Juvenile literature. [1. Stowe, Harriet Beecher, 1811-1896. 2. Authors, American.]
I. Title. II. Series.
PS2956.A94 1990
813'.3—dc20
[B]
[92]   89-25364
                     CIP
                     AC

PHOTO CREDITS

The Bettmann Archive—22 (left), 25, 26 (left)
Essex Institute, Salem, Massachusetts—22 (right)
Historical Pictures Service, Chicago—Cover (both images), 1, 2, 15 (top left), 15 (top right), 21 (right), 26 (right), 31 (top right), 32 (left)
Northwind Picture Archives—7 (right), 12, 15 (bottom right), 15 (bottom left), 16, 17, 18, 19, 20, 21 (left), 23, 24 (2 photos), 31 (bottom right)
© Jim Scourletis—32 (right)
Stowe-Day Foundation—4, 7 (left), 9 (2 photos), 10, 11, 28, 31 (left)
Virginia State Library—13

You are eleven years old. Your brother is two. Your mother is holding you both so tightly that you can hear how fast her heart is beating. She's scared and so are you. You're at a slave auction. You are going to be sold.

Men walk up to your mother and examine her teeth, feel her arms and legs, thump her on the back. Sometimes they do the same to you and your brother. Some of the men are rough with you, others are more gentle. Quietly your mother begs, "Please, sir, buy us all together. Please. We'll work hard." Some shake their heads, some look away. Some laugh. No one listens.

When it is time for you to be sold, you stand on the auction block with your mother and brother. You don't like to have so many people looking at you. Your mother starts screaming. Two men are tearing your brother from her arms. You try to help her, but the auctioneer's helper knocks you down. Another man kicks you to your feet. He is your new master. Your mother has been sold to someone else. You don't see who got your brother. You watch as your mother is dragged away. You can hear your brother calling, "Mama! Mama!" You will never see him or your mother again. You look up at your new master, but he has already forgotten you and is watching the bidding. Someone chains you to the line of other slaves your new master has bought that day.

Scenes like this took place every day in the United States of America for almost three hundred years. Some people thought there was nothing wrong with slavery. Some people thought it was a necessary evil. Others risked their lives and died trying to change it. In the end, however, no one did as much as one small woman who knew how it felt to lose a child. Harriet Beecher Stowe wrote a book called *Uncle Tom's Cabin*, and nearly everyone who read it was changed by her words. After Harriet's death, the poet Paul Laurence Dunbar wrote a sonnet about her. These are the last two lines:

Prophet and Priestess! At one stroke she gave
    A race to freedom, and herself to fame.

This is the story of a remarkable woman—Harriet Beecher Stowe.

Left: Lyman Beecher. Right: Birthplace of Harriet Beecher Stowe in Litchfield, Connecticut.

Lyman Beecher wasn't very excited about his new baby girl. He wanted sons! Sons were important because they could grow up to be preachers like their father. Girls weren't capable of much, and now he had three of them. At least he had three sons, too. He sighed and agreed with his wife, Roxana, that they should name the new baby Harriet, after Roxana's sister. He entered the baby's name and date of birth in the family Bible: Harriet Elizabeth Beecher, born June 14, 1811.

The Beecher family lived in Litchfield, Connecticut, in a big old house that they liked—except for the rats. No matter how many rats Lyman Beecher shot, trapped, or left to the cats, there were always more. "Where did they all come from?" the Beechers wondered. And the rats must have wondered the same thing about the Beechers.

Besides Roxana and Lyman and their total of eight children, six other people lived in the house — relatives, boarders, and servants. The Beecher children had pets, too. It was a busy house. And it was a pleasant place to grow up.

Harriet's Aunt Esther lived with the Beechers, and she knew dozens of stories about the animals in the woods and fields around them. Harriet's father was strict, but he didn't have many rules. Mostly he was an adventure in himself. Harriet and her sisters and brothers could never be sure what the new day would bring. Their father might call them bright and early to come and pick chestnuts or apples with him. Or his stomach could be bothering him and he'd gather his children around to tell them that the end was near. It made him feel better to have them cry for him, and usually the next day he was rounding them up for a picnic or an expedition.

Harriet's mother died when Harriet was five years old. It was a terrible tragedy for the family, and the eight Beecher children remembered their gentle, beautiful mother until they died themselves.

Right: Catharine Beecher, Harriet's sister, established schools for women in Hartford, Connecticut, and Cincinnati, Ohio. Left: Harriet's brother Henry Ward Beecher became a famous preacher.

Their Aunt Esther took over the household, and much as they loved her, her passion for neatness and order was hard for the careless and disorganized Beechers to take. When their father remarried after a year, they were all secretly relieved to have their supervision shift from Aunt Esther to their new stepmother.

Harriet's father became a famous preacher. His sermons were published and distributed throughout New England. Harriet's older brothers followed in his footsteps. Harriet's sister Catharine started a school for women in Hartford, Connecticut. She was becoming a well-known educator.

No one paid much attention to little Harriet. She never grew taller than five feet, and though she loved to make faces to amuse her brothers, she was usually quiet and thoughtful. So thoughtful, in fact, that she seemed to be in a trance sometimes, and her brothers said she was "owling about." She had an amazing memory. All the Beecher children had to memorize Bible verses and hymns. At the age of five, Harriet knew twenty-seven hymns and two long chapters of the Bible by heart. When she was thirteen years old, Harriet was sent to Hartford to attend her sister's school.

Hartford Female Seminary

Before long, Harriet was teaching as well as studying at the Hartford Female Seminary. Every year she taught more classes until finally she was a full-time teacher. She didn't enjoy teaching, but it was hard to argue with her strong-minded sister.

It was hard to argue with her father, too. In fact, Harriet didn't even try. After he was offered an important position in Cincinnati, Ohio, all the Beecher children moved west, too. Harriet was twenty-one years old.

The Beecher family

Catharine Beecher started a school in Cincinnati—the Western Female Institute. Harriet dutifully took her place there as a teacher. Then Catharine asked Harriet to write a geography book for children. The book was published in March 1833—but Catharine was named as the author! It would sell better that way, Harriet was told. Catharine was well known, and her name would help sell the book.

Cincinnati was different from New England towns and cities. Harriet found it hard to get used to

The bustling riverfront of Cincinnati, Ohio, in 1866

$100 REWARD!

I will give the above reward for a runa-way named LEWIS, belonging to the estate of Joseph Thompson, dec'd., if he is apprehended out of State of Virginia, or $50 if apprehended in this State, provided he is delivered to me or secured in jail so that I get him.

LEWIS ran off in the month of September last, from Thomas G. Marshall, who resides near Farrowsville, in Fauquier County, and to whom he was hired for 1854. He has many acquaintances and connexions in the neighborhood of White Ridge, in Fauquier County, where he was raised, and is probably lurking in that vicinity, or he may have obtained employment in Loudoun county as a free man.

Lewis is about 5 feet 11 inches high, of black complexion, has good teeth, inclined to be spare, but is well made and likely. He is about 25 years old.

JOHN P. PHILIPS,
Administrator of Joseph Thompson, dec'd.

Warrenton, Va.

Slave owners often distributed posters like the one above, advertising a reward for the return of a runaway slave.

the roughness and filth of a booming frontier city. One thing she never got used to was seeing posters offering a reward for the return of a runaway slave.

Cincinnati was across the Ohio River from Kentucky. People in Kentucky could own slaves. People in Ohio could not. Harriet and the rest of the Beechers had always known about slavery, and they had always believed it was wrong. But it was easy, in New England, not to think about people being bought and sold and made to work against their will. In Cincinnati, it was not so easy. Harriet met and talked with former slaves and with people who were working to end slavery. She also met people who believed that slavery was a perfectly good idea. Her brother Charles went to work in Louisiana for a year, and he told Harriet about the calaboose, a place where slave owners could send their slaves to be whipped by professionals. Expert floggers could cut off a piece of a slave's flesh with each lash of the whip. Charles told Harriet about plantations with such rich soil and such unhealthy climates that it was cheaper for the master to work his slaves to death than to take care of them.

Once Harriet was invited to a student's home in Kentucky. The girl lived on a plantation. Harriet couldn't forget the little slave cabins and the sight of slaves working in the fields.

In the Cincinnati newspaper, Harriet read about a lawsuit between two men—Meek and Phillips. Meek was a slave owner, and he'd hired Phillips to make his slaves work harder. One day Phillips whipped one of Meek's young slave boys to death. Meek took Phillips to court. The court agreed that Phillips should pay Meek the price of the slave boy. No one thought Phillips should be punished for murdering the child. Slaves were simply possessions—things that were owned. Harriet listened and watched and remembered.

HEWLETT & BRIGHT.

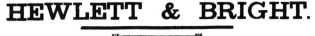

SALE OF

VALUABLE
SLAVES,

(On account of departure)

The Owner of the following named and valuable Slaves, being on the eve of departure for Europe, will cause the same to be offered for sale, at the NEW EXCHANGE, corner of St. Louis and Chartres streets, on *Saturday,* May 16, at Twelve o'Clock, *viz.*

1. **SARAH,** a mulatress, aged 45 years, a good cook and accustomed to house work in general, is an excellent and faithful nurse for sick persons, and in every respect a first rate character.

2. **DENNIS,** her son, a mulatto, aged 24 years, a first rate cook and steward for a vessel, having been in that capacity for many years on board one of the Mobile packets; is strictly honest, temperate, and a first rate subject.

3. **CHOLE,** a mulatress, aged 36 years, she is, without exception, one of the most competent servants in the country, a first rate washer and ironer, does up lace, a good cook, and for a bachelor who wishes a house-keeper she would be invaluable; she is also a good ladies' maid, having travelled to the North in that capacity.

4. **FANNY,** her daughter, a mulatress, aged 16 years, speaks French and English, is a superior hair-dresser, (pupil of Guilliac,) a good seamstress and ladies' maid, is smart, intelligent, and a first rate character.

5. **DANDRIDGE,** a mulatoo, aged 26 years, a first rate dining-room servant, a good painter and rough carpenter, and has but few equals for honesty and sobriety.

6. **NANCY,** his wife, aged about 24 years, a confidential house servant, good seamstress, mantuamaker and tailoress, a good cook, washer and ironer, etc.

7. **MARY ANN,** her child, a creole, aged 7 years, speaks French and English, is smart, active and intelligent.

8. **FANNY or FRANCES,** a mulatress, aged 22 years, is a first rate washer and ironer, good cook and house servant, and has an excellent character.

9. **EMMA,** an orphan, aged 10 or 11 years, speaks French and English, has been in the country 7 years, has been accustomed to waiting on table, sewing etc.; is intelligent and active.

10. **FRANK,** a mulatto, aged about 32 years speaks French and English, is a first rate hostler and coachman, understands perfectly well the management of horses, and is, in every respect, a first rate character, with the exception that he will occasionally drink, though not an habitual drunkard.

☞ All the above named Slaves are acclimated and excellent subjects; they were purchased by their present vendor many years ago, and will, therefore, be severally warranted against all vices and maladies prescribed by law, save and except FRANK, who is fully guaranteed in every other respect but the one above mentioned.

TERMS:—One-half Cash, and the other half in notes at Six months, drawn and endorsed to the satisfaction of the Vendor, with special mortgage on the Slaves until final payment. The Acts of Sale to be passed before WILLIAM BOSWELL, *Notary Public,* at the expense of the Purchaser.

New-Orleans, May 13, 1835.

Left: An advertisement for a slave auction in New Orleans in 1835. Family members might be sold to different owners and separated forever.

A Sugar Plantation.

Bowdoin College in Brunswick, Maine, in the 1840s

In 1836 Harriet married Calvin Stowe. Calvin was a professor of theology at Lane Theological Seminary in Cincinnati. His salary wasn't enough for their growing family, and Harriet struggled to make ends meet. She loved their children deeply and fiercely, and when cholera killed her baby, Charley, in 1849, Harriet wrote, "I have just seen him in his death agony, looked on his imploring face when I could not help nor soothe nor do one thing, not one, to mitigate his cruel suffering—do nothing but pray in my anguish that he might die soon."

She had never liked Cincinnati. Now she hated it. When Calvin was offered a position at Bowdoin College in Brunswick, Maine, Harriet was glad to go.

She had been earning money for the family by writing magazine articles, and now she worked even harder to earn money for the move.

In Brunswick, Harriet gave birth to her sixth and last child. The Stowe family was poorer than ever. Harriet wrote as much as possible, between taking care of the house and the children.

Then came the news that Congress had passed the Fugitive Slave Act. The new law said that people who helped slaves to escape could be punished by the government. Harriet remembered the young black woman she had hired as a servant in Cincinnati. The woman had said she was a freed slave. One day she came to Harriet in tears, confessing that she had run

Areas of freedom and slavery in 1857

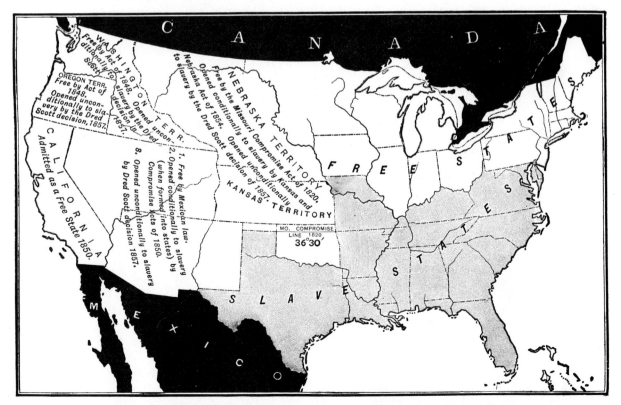

These two fugitive slaves were recaptured in Boston under the Fugitive Slave Act. They were returned to slavery in South Carolina.

away and now her master was in Cincinnati, looking for her. She begged Harriet for help. Harriet and Calvin took her to people who could help the young woman make her way to freedom in Canada. Had she and Calvin been wrong? Harriet knew they were not wrong. The Fugitive Slave Act was an unjust law.

But it was a law all the same, and now slave hunters could be found even in New England. Black people were being dragged off the streets of Boston. Harriet's brother's wife wrote to her, "Hattie, if I could use a pen as you can, I would write something that will make this whole nation feel what an accursed thing slavery is." Harriet read the letter to her children, then crumpled it in her hand. "I *will* write something," she said, her voice shaking. "I will if I live."

A few weeks later, Harriet was sitting in church when a vivid picture sprang into her mind. She saw a brave, strong, gentle black man being whipped to death by two other slaves as their white slave owner watched. Harriet walked home from church and wrote down what she had seen. She called the brave man Uncle Tom. The other two slaves were Sambo and Quimbo, and the cruel owner was Simon Legree.

Harriet knew she had to write the story of Uncle Tom. She decided to write it as a serial for an anti-slavery magazine called the *National Era*. She thought it would take three or four weeks to write the story.

Later, Harriet said that God had written *Uncle Tom's Cabin*. All she had to do was pick up her pen and the words poured out, she claimed. All the same,

Part of the handwritten manuscript of *Uncle Tom's Cabin* by Harriet Beecher Stowe

The house in Brunswick, Maine, where *Uncle Tom's Cabin* was written

it was difficult simply to find time to pick up her pen. She had six children. One of them was a new baby. She had a house to run, and there were no washing machines or vacuum cleaners or dishwashers in those days. Food was cooked on a wood-burning stove. Water had to be carried into the house and heated for washing and bathing. Harriet continued to write, her story grew longer and longer, and still it was not near being finished. It took a year to tell Uncle Tom's story.

Everything Harriet had seen or read or heard about slavery found its way into her book. She couldn't forget her little Charley and how hard it had been to lose him. She used her own tragedy to make people understand how it felt for slaves to lose their children to the highest bidder.

Harriet had heard the economic arguments that supported slavery. She knew of kind slave owners and contented slaves. She knew people who hated slavery but would never welcome a black person into their community. All of these different people could see themselves in Harriet's book. Harriet painted pictures with words, and people could not forget what they saw.

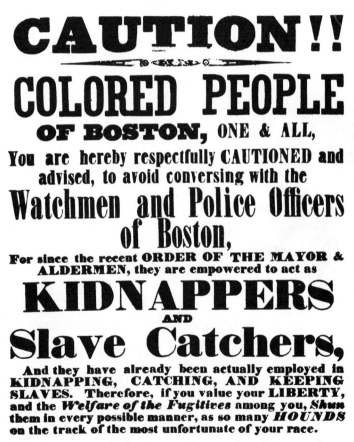

Above: Harriet Beecher Stowe in 1852. Right: Blacks were warned about slave catchers by posters issued in Boston.

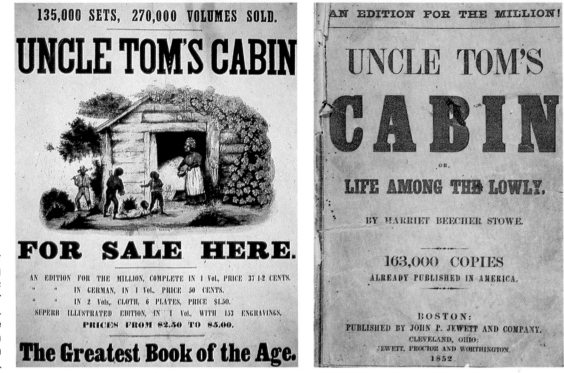

Left: A poster advertising *Uncle Tom's Cabin* for sale.
Right: The cover of an 1852 edition of the book.

Soon after Harriet's story was completed in the *National Era*, it was published as a book by Jewett & Company, a Boston publisher. Mr. Jewett had been persuaded to take a chance on the book by his wife, who'd followed the story in the magazine. He printed five thousand copies. Harriet hoped to make enough money to buy a new dress.

The first day the book was available in stores, three thousand copies were sold. The rest were sold the next day. The publisher printed more copies. Twenty thousand copies sold in three weeks. At Jewett's publishing house, the presses couldn't keep up. Three mills worked to make enough paper to print the book. Nothing like *Uncle Tom's Cabin* had ever been printed in the United States before.

Then people in other countries wanted the book. Soon British publishers were selling copies, and it was translated into other languages. People all over the world read *Uncle Tom's Cabin* and rose up against slavery.

The book made money, and Harriet was glad to have escaped from poverty for the first time in her life. But she was happiest that people who read her book learned something about what it was like to be a slave. That was the most important thing.

No one claimed that *Uncle Tom's Cabin* was great literature. It was too sentimental, for one thing, and

There were two ways for blacks to escape from slavery: They could run away (inset), or they could be released by death.

Left: Harriet with Henry Ward Beecher in the 1860s. Right: The Reverend Josiah Henson, a slave who may have given Harriet the idea for Uncle Tom.

Harriet, the preacher's daughter, made parts of it sound like a sermon. Also, she'd written it in such a hurry that she hadn't paid close attention to grammar and punctuation. Even so, the characters in the book seemed real and believable, and people laughed and cried along with them.

In *Uncle Tom's Cabin*, Tom is a gentle, strong, religious slave belonging to the Shelby family, who own a plantation in Kentucky. Tom and his wife, Chloe, have three small children. They live in one of the Shelbys' slave cabins.

In the large plantation house, Mrs. Shelby has a beautiful maid named Eliza, who is also a slave. Eliza has a small boy named Harry.

This theater poster for an 1899 "Tom show" depicts Eliza's dramatic escape from the slave trader.

One day Eliza overhears Mr. Shelby arranging with a slave trader for the sale of Tom and her son Harry. That night she takes her child and, first stopping at Tom's cabin to warn him, runs to the north. She gets to the Ohio River by morning, just as the slave trader tracks her down. The river is full of broken ice—no one will take a boat out to be crushed by the grinding floes. Eliza sees the slave trader, picks up her child, and crosses the river by jumping from ice floe to ice floe. On the other side, she is helped by a number of people and even reunited with her husband.

In the meantime, Chloe begs Tom to run away, too. He refuses, telling her that if he is not there to be sold, others may have to be sold in his place. In the morning, Tom is taken away from his wife and children forever.

Tom's new master intends to sell him at the slave market in New Orleans. They travel by steamboat down the Mississippi River, and Tom sees one tragic scene after another as slaves are bought and added to his master's group. One day, Tom saves a little white girl from drowning. She begs her father to buy Tom for her, and he does so. The beautiful little girl's name is Eva, and her father is Augustine St.

Uncle Tom was bought by St. Clare after saving little Eva's life. Right: In an illustration from a German edition, Uncle Tom stands up to Simon Legree.

Clare. Tom and Eva spend hours reading the Bible together, and Eva asks her father to make out the papers to free Tom. Eva dies of tuberculosis. In his grief, St. Clare doesn't complete Tom's free papers. Soon St. Clare dies, too. Tom must be sold again.

At the slave auction, Tom is sold to Simon Legree, a cruel man who hopes to teach Tom to be an overseer on his farm. Legree finds it cheaper to work his slaves to death and buy new ones when he needs them. He keeps his slaves like animals, feeding them poorly and making them sleep in filthy sheds.

Legree orders Tom to whip a slave—a sick, older woman. Tom refuses. Legree orders Sambo and Quimbo, his two black overseers, to whip Tom. Later, when Tom refuses to tell Legree where two runaway slaves are hiding, Legree has Tom beaten again. Tom begs Legree not to do it. "O, Mas'r! Don't bring this great sin on your soul! It will hurt you more than t'will hurt me! Do the worst you can, my troubles will be over soon; but, if ye don't repent, yours won't *never* end!" Legree doesn't listen. This time he has Tom beaten to death.

As Tom lies dying, George Shelby, the son of the owner of the Kentucky plantation, arrives to buy Tom back. Tom begs him not to tell Chloe how he died. George stays till Tom dies, then buries him and returns home to free all his slaves.

People in the South insisted that the book was a pack of lies. The book was banned there, and other books were written to show how wrong it was. None of them were taken seriously. Harriet received threatening letters. One day, the Stowes opened a package addressed to them and out fell a human ear. It had been cut from the head of a slave.

Years later, Harriet met President Abraham Lincoln at the White House. President Lincoln took her small hand and said, "So this is the little lady who made this big war?"

Harriet, shown here with President Lincoln, met many influential people after she became world famous.

Had Harriet caused the war? She didn't like to think she was responsible for so much suffering. But her book had drawn so much attention to the injustice of slavery that people had found themselves unable to forget or ignore it as they had before. An economic depression in 1857 had brought hard times to both Northern and Southern states. Bad feelings simmered on both sides. The Southern states felt that they were being treated unfairly by the government.

In the presidential election of 1860, Abraham Lincoln received the most votes. He had promised in his campaign to preserve the Union and free the slaves. A group of Southern states vowed to secede from the Union if Lincoln became president, and a month after his inauguration in March 1861, they did. The Southern states called their new nation the Confederate States of America.

The Civil War began in April 1861, when Confederate troops fired on Fort Sumter in South Carolina. It ended in 1865, after hundreds of thousands of people had been killed. Harriet's own son Fred was injured and never completely recovered. The nation was scarred, but the slaves were free and the Union was intact.

Harriet's book had changed the world in a way that few other books have.

Even after the war, people continued to read *Uncle Tom's Cabin.* Many people put on plays based on the book. In these plays, Uncle Tom was usually portrayed as being very old, stupid, happy-go-lucky, and obedient. Often he rode around on a donkey and looked as foolish as possible. These plays gave people a false idea of what black people were like. Black people began to hate the book that had helped to set them free. To be called an "Uncle Tom" became a terrible insult. In 1963, a woman in Akron, Ohio, sued a newspaper for libel after it called her an "Uncle Tom." She won the case and $32,000 in damages.

Harriet Beecher Stowe could not have foreseen that her book would have such an impact on the world for so long. She had hoped to strike a blow against slavery and to earn some money for her family. She was wildly successful on both counts. After her book was published, she was welcomed by presidents, kings, and queens all over the world. She continued to write books, and all of them became best sellers. She and Calvin traveled and enjoyed their family. Calvin died in 1886. Harriet died in 1896, at the age of 85. She is buried in the Andover Chapel cemetery in Andover, Massachusetts.

The many stage productions of *Uncle Tom's Cabin* distorted the character of Tom into a simple-minded buffoon. The blacks (lower right) celebrating the abolition of slavery in Washington, D.C., had probably never read Harriet Beecher Stowe's (top right) remarkable book.

Harriet Beecher Stowe spent her last years in a house she built in Hartford, Connecticut. A stone cross (right) marks her grave.

INDEX

About the Author

Maureen Ash grew up riding horses and reading books in Milaca, Minnesota. She likes cross-country skiing, swimming, and roller blading. She has a blue house, a big garden, a small daughter, and a long, narrow cat.

#9.95